Eye Color: Brown, Blue, Green, and Other Hues

Jennifer Boothroyd

Lerner Publications Company
Minneapolis

W9-BPJ-201

For Emily and her sparkling eyes
—J.B.

Lerner Publications Company
A division of Lerner Publishing Group, Inc.
241 First Avenue North
Minneapolis, MN 55401 U.S.A.

Website address: www.lernerbooks.com

Library of Congress Cataloging-in-Publication Data

Boothroyd, Jennifer, 1972–
    Eye color : brown, blue, green, and other hues / by Jennifer Boothroyd.
       p.   cm. — (Lightning bolt books™ — What traits are in your genes?)
    Includes bibliographical references and index.
    ISBN 978-0-7613-8938-5 (lib. bdg : alk. paper)
    1. Genetics—Juvenile literature. 2. Heredity—Juvenile literature. 3. Color of eyes—Juvenile literature. I. Title.
    QH437.5.B66 2013
    572.8—dc23   2011039376

Manufactured in the United States of America
1 — CG — 7/15/12

Table of Contents

Genes

Humans look similar. We all have the same basic parts.

All these kids have eyes, ears, and noses—just like you!

But humans have differences too.

Look closely. All kids don't look the same.

These differences are called traits.

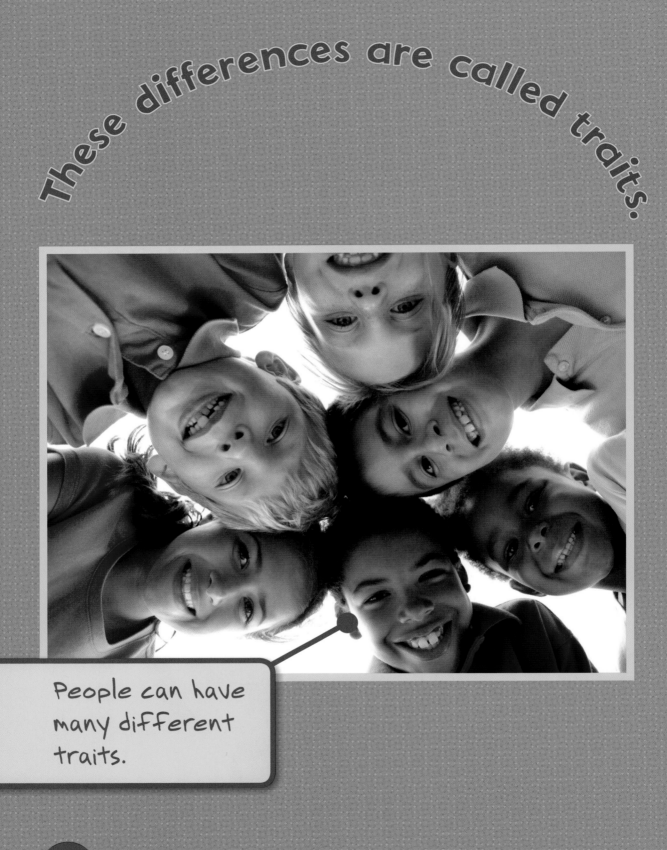

People can have many different traits.

Hair color is a trait. So are dimples and freckles.

Do you have freckles? Freckles are a trait.

Genes tell your body how to make different traits. Genes are like instructions for the body.

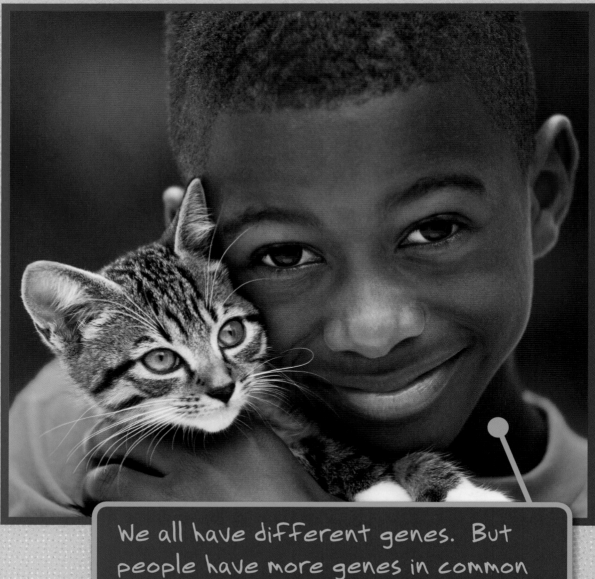

We all have different genes. But people have more genes in common with one another than they do with cats or other animals.

Birth parents pass on genes to kids.

Birth parents are related to their children. Adoptive parents take a child into their family and become his or her parents.

You have two copies of each of your genes. One copy came from each parent.

These kids got copies of their genes from both of their parents.

Your parents' genes might give you straight hair. They might give you curly hair. They control whether your hair is dark or light.

This girl got genes for curly hair. Her brother got genes for straight hair.

Eye Color

What color are your eyes? Your genes control your eye color.

Take a look at the people around you. How many eye colors do you see?

People have many different eye colors. The colored ring in your eyes is called the iris.

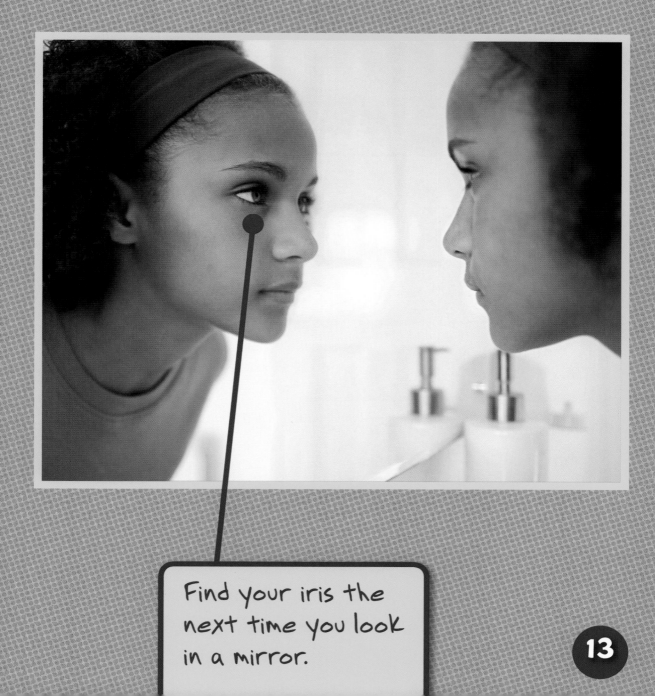

Find your iris the next time you look in a mirror.

Pigment in the iris gives eyes their color.

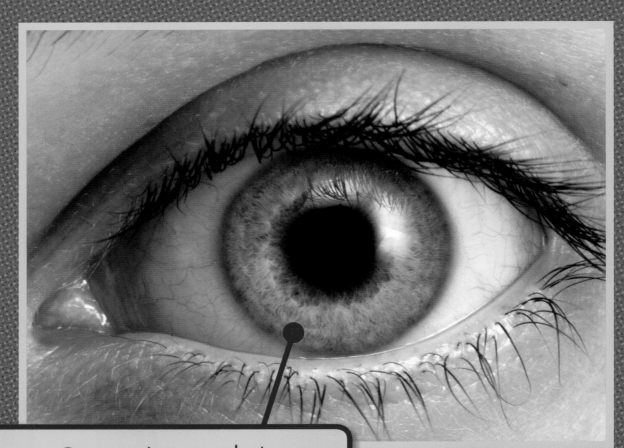

Pigment is a substance that gives color to something. Skin has pigment too.

Pigment also protects eyes from light.

Those with light-colored eyes can be more sensitive to light. Their eyes have less pigment to protect them.

Brown Eyes

Genes come in different forms, called alleles. Your mom might give you a blue-eyed allele. Your dad might give you a brown-eyed allele.

How does your body know which one to use?

What eye color will these future parents give their baby?

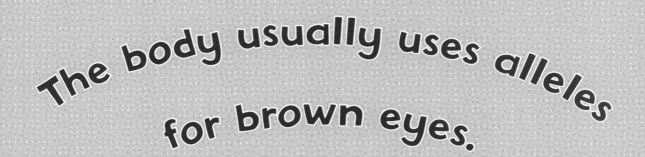

The body usually uses alleles for brown eyes.

Most people have brown eyes.

Why does the body usually use alleles for brown eyes?

It's because they are dominant. That means they are stronger than other alleles.

Strong brown-eyed alleles gave this child brown eyes.

Brown-eyed parents can have kids with other eye colors.

The members of this family have many different eye colors.

This happens when the parents have alleles for both brown eyes and other colors. They might pass on alleles for colors other than brown.

This child's parents passed on green-eyed alleles.

Blue and Other Hues

Blue and green eyes are not as common as brown eyes. But you probably have friends with these eye colors. Or maybe you have them yourself.

Do you know someone with blue or green eyes?

Eyes come in other hues too. Gray eyes have less pigment than blue eyes.

Gray eyes are lighter than blue eyes.

Amber eyes have less pigment than brown.

Amber is an orangey-yellow shade.

Hazel eyes are a mixture of green and brown.

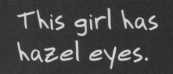
This girl has hazel eyes.

24

The alleles that make these colors are recessive. Recessive alleles are weaker than dominant alleles.

Both parents in this family passed blue-eyed alleles on to their child.

Eye color is one of many traits made by genes. Genes are passed from parent to child for generations.

Genes are passed from grandparents to parents to children.

This scientist studies genes to learn more about the human body.

Scientists are still learning about genes. Their findings help them understand the human body.

Activity
Track the Traits!

Track the different eye colors in your classroom. List these eye colors on a sheet of lined paper:

amber	brown	green
blue	gray	hazel

Then divide your paper into two columns. One column will be for the eye colors. The other column will be for tally marks. (You'll find out what tally marks are and how to use them next.) Your paper should look like the sample sheet on page 29 when you're done.

Put a tally mark next to the eye color that you have. A tally mark is a straight up-and-down line, like this:

|

Then ask your classmates about their eye color. Make a tally mark for each classmate next to his or her eye color. When you get to five, put a diagonal line through your tally marks, like this:

||||

That's how you write the number five in tally marks. For the number six, make a new tally mark, like this:

$$\text{IIII I}$$

When you're done tallying the eye colors, count how many of you have each color. Which color got the most tallies?

Sample Sheet:

Eye Colors	Tally Marks
amber	
blue	
brown	
gray	
green	
hazel	

Glossary

allele: one of two or more forms of a gene

birth parent: a parent that is genetically related to his or her child

dominant: most powerful or the strongest

gene: one of the parts of the cells of all living things. Genes are passed from parents to children and determine how you look and the way you grow.

hue: a color or a variety of a color

iris: the round, colored part of the eye

pigment: a substance that gives color to something

recessive: less powerful or weaker

trait: a quality or characteristic that makes one person or thing different from another

Further Reading

American Museum of Natural History: The Gene Scene
http://www.amnh.org/ology/genetics

Boothroyd, Jennifer. *What Is Sight?* Minneapolis: Lerner Publications Company, 2010.

The Geee! in Genome
http://nature.ca/genome/04/041/041_e.cfm

Harris, Trudy. *Tally Cat Keeps Track*. Minneapolis: Millbrook Press, 2011.

Klingel, Cynthia, and Robert B. Noyed. *Eyes.* New York: Gareth Stevens, 2010.

Tour of the Basics: What Is a Trait?
http://learn.genetics.utah.edu/content/begin/traits/tour_trait.html

Weiss, Ellen. *The Sense of Sight.* New York: Children's Press, 2009.

Index

Photo Acknowledgments

The images in this book are used with the permission of: © Anna Peisl/CORBIS, p. 1; © KidStock/Blend Images/Getty Images, p. 2; © Monkey Business Images/Dreamstime.com, pp. 4, 5, 6, 10, 31 © Uwe Krejci/The Image Bank/Getty Images, p. 7; © Arthur Tilley/Workbook Stock/Getty Images, p. 8; © Dennis Wise/Photodisc/Getty Images, p. 9; © Ariel Skelley/Blend Images/Getty Images, p. 11; © Sergiy Nykonenko/Dreamstime.com, p. 12; © Roy McMahon/Digital Vision/Getty Images, p. 13; © Oxford Scientific/Getty Images, p. 14; © Darrin Klimek/Taxi/Getty Images, p. 15; © Yuri Arcurs/Dreamstime.com, p. 16; © Zurijeta/Dreamstime.com, p. 17; © Shuttlecock/Dreamstime.com, p. 18; © Wavebreakmedia Ltd./Dreamstime.com, p. 19; © Goodluz/Dreamstime.com, p. 20; © Manchan/Photodisc/Getty Images, p. 21; © DCA Productions/Taxi/Getty Images, p. 22; © Robert Houser/Photodisc/Getty Images, p. 23; © Jupiterimages/Botanica/Getty Images, p. 24; © Even Kafka/The Image Bank/Getty Images, p. 25; © Comstock Images/Getty Images, p. 26; © Bloomberg via Getty Images, p. 27; © Brand New Images/Stone/Getty Images, p. 30.

Front cover: © Eyecandy Images/Glow Images (left); © Stefan Hermans/Dreamstime.com (right).

Main body text set in Johann Light 30/36.